Wild Animal

DOLPHINS

GAIL TERP

**BLACK
RABBIT
BOOKS**

Bolt is published by Black Rabbit Books
P.O. Box 3263, Mankato, Minnesota, 56002.
www.blackrabbitbooks.com
Copyright © 2018 Black Rabbit Books

Jennifer Besel, editor; Grant Gould, interior
designer; Michael Sellner, cover designer;
Omay Ayres, photo researcher

Library of Congress Cataloging-in-Publication Data
Names: Terp, Gail, 1951- author.
Title: Dolphins / by Gail Terp.
Description: Mankato, Minnesota : Black Rabbit Books, [2018] | Series:
Bolt. Wild animal kingdom | Audience: Age 9-12. | Audience: Grade 4 to 6.
| Includes bibliographical references and index.
Identifiers: LCCN 2016049993 (print) | LCCN 2017005162 (ebook) | ISBN
9781680721881 (library binding) | ISBN 9781680722529 (ebook) | ISBN
9781680724851 (paperback)
Subjects: LCSH: Dolphins–Juvenile literature.
Classification: LCC QL737.C432 T46 2018 (print) | LCC QL737.C432
(ebook) | DDC 599.53–dc23
LC record available at https://lccn.loc.gov/2016049993

Printed in the United States at CG Book Printers,
North Mankato, Minnesota, 56003. 3/17

Image Credits

Getty Images: Barcroft/Barcroft
Media, 4–5; Stockbyte, 27 (top); iStock:
Sethakan, 6; National Geographic Creative:
DAVID DOUBILET, 27 (bottom); Shutterstock:
3DMI, 29 (shark); Andrea Izzotti, 22 (top), 24;
Christian Musat, 29 (killer whale); Elena Larina, 18–
19; Eric Isselee, 29 (seal); Four Oaks, 23 (bottom); Jarp2,
32; MANSILIYA YURY, 29 (fish); Neirfy, 14–15 (dolphin),
29 (dolphin); Rich Carey, 26; Schalke fotografie|Melissa
Schalke, Cover; SiiKA Photo, 8–9, 31; Steve Noakes, Back
Cover, 1; stockphoto mania, 22–23; Targn Pleiades, 11;
Tory Kallman, 12; tsuneomp, 17; Volosina, 29 (squid);
Willyam Bradberry, 3, 20; ylq, 21 (both)
Every effort has been made to contact copyright
holders for material reproduced in this book.
Any omissions will be rectified in subse-
quent printings if notice is given
to the publisher.

BOLT

Contents

CHAPTER 1

A Day in the Life

    A **pod** of dolphins is on a hunt. The animals use sounds to **communicate** with each other. The sounds are like whistles and clicks.

    A school of fish is just ahead. The dolphins circle the fish. Round and round they swim. They herd the fish into a small ball. While some keep herding, the other dolphins feed. Then they switch, so all can eat.

COMPARING SIZES

		FEET	0	2

Hector's dolphin
4.5 FEET (1 meter)
110 POUNDS
(50 kilograms)

bottlenose dolphin
8 FEET (2 meters)
600 POUNDS
(272 kilograms)

killer whale
20 FEET (6 meters)
10,000 POUNDS
(4,536 kilograms)

POUNDS 0 1,000

The Dolphin Family

There are about 40 types of dolphins. Some are small. Others are huge. But they are all **mammals**. They can't breathe underwater. They must come to the surface to breathe. They breathe through their blowholes.

The names of some dolphins can be confusing. Some are called whales. The largest dolphins are killer whales.

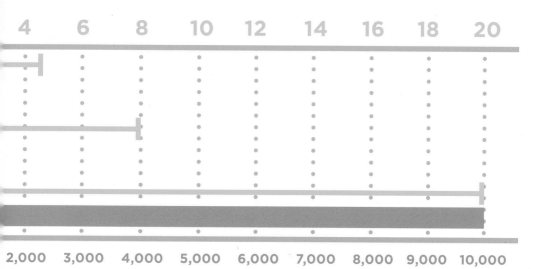

DOLPHIN FEATURES

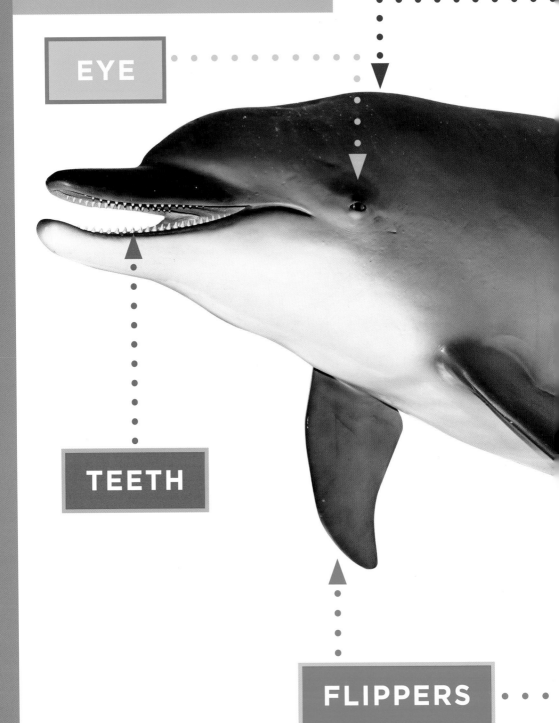

EYE

TEETH

FLIPPERS

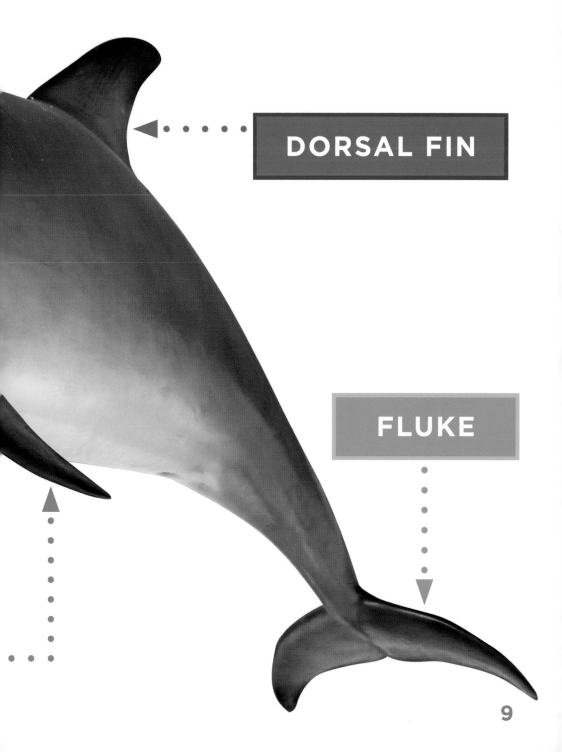

BLOWHOLE

DORSAL FIN

FLUKE

9

CHAPTER 2

Food to Eat
and a Place to Live

Most dolphins eat fish and squid. Large dolphins also eat large **prey**, such as seals. Dolphins eat up to 50 pounds (23 kg) of food a day.

Dolphins use **echolocation** to hunt. They make clicks in the water. The sounds hit prey and bounce back. By listening to the echoes, dolphins know where prey is.

A Home in the World

Dolphins live in nearly all oceans. But they don't live near the North or South Poles. Many live near **shallow** coasts. Some live in the open sea. Other dolphins live in large rivers.

A dolphin never completely sleeps. One side of its brain stays awake. One eye stays open to watch for danger.

Dolphin Range Map

CHAPTER 3

Family Life

Dolphins live in pods. Small pods can have two to 40 dolphins. Large pods have more than 1,000 dolphins. Pod sizes depend on how much food is in an area. The more food there is, the larger the pod.

Keeping in Touch

Dolphins communicate with whistles and other sounds. With sounds, dolphins tell others where prey is. They also warn each other of danger. And when they want to play, sounds tell that too.

Dolphins do not have a sense of smell.

COMPARING
SIZES
of bottlenose
dolphins

Calves

Dolphin mothers give birth every two to six years. Most have one calf. Twins are **rare**. Calves stay with their mothers for up to eight years. Then the calves can hunt for themselves.

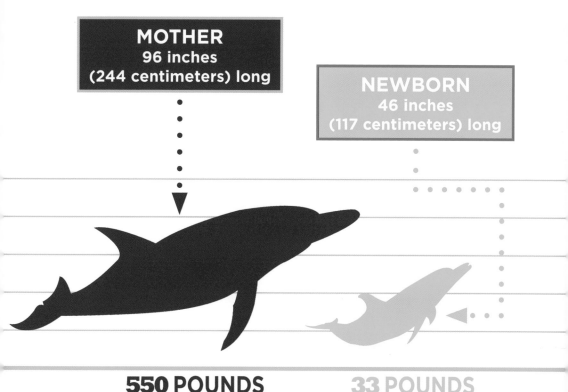

MOTHER
96 inches
(244 centimeters) long

NEWBORN
46 inches
(117 centimeters) long

550 POUNDS
(249 kg)

33 POUNDS
(15 kg)

By the Numbers

up to 90 YEARS
LIFE SPAN

up to 104
NUMBER OF TEETH
IN A BOTTLENOSE
DOLPHIN'S MOUTH

25 MILES
(40 kilometers)
PER HOUR

TOP SWIMMING SPEED

about 100,000

NUMBER OF
DOLPHINS IN BIGGEST
POD EVER SEEN

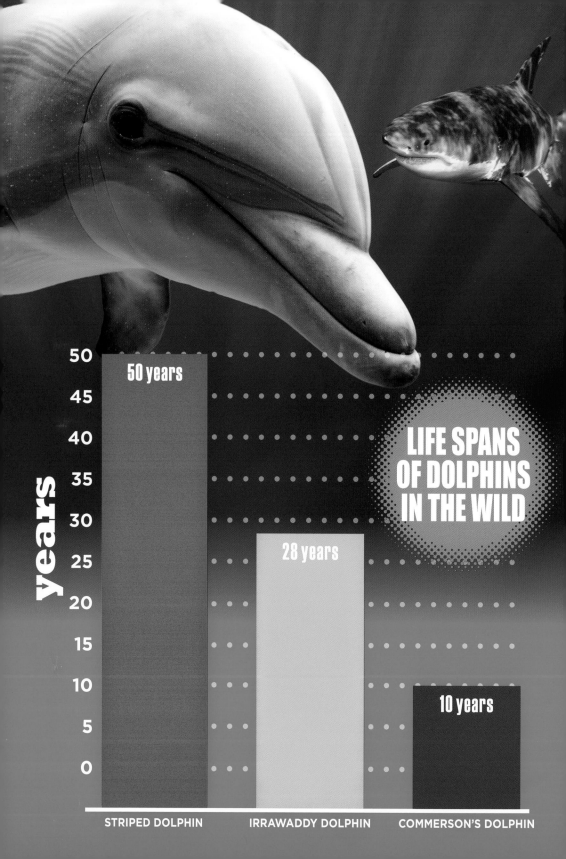

LIFE SPANS OF DOLPHINS IN THE WILD

years

50 — **50 years**
45
40
35
30
25 — **28 years**
20
15
10 — **10 years**
5
0

STRIPED DOLPHIN   IRRAWADDY DOLPHIN   COMMERSON'S DOLPHIN

CHAPTER 4

Predators
and Other Threats

Large adult dolphins have few **predators**. Killer whales eat other dolphins. Sharks prey on dolphins too. But traveling in pods keeps dolphins safer. Many sharks avoid dolphins.

Threats to Dolphins

Humans put some dolphins at risk. Their actions cause dolphins to get sick. They cause many to die. At least nine types of dolphins are in danger of **extinction**.

Pollution

Dirty water makes dolphins sick.

Hurting Dolphins

Fishing Nets

Dolphins get caught in nets and drown.

Hunting

Some people hunt dolphins for food.

Protection

To protect dolphins, people have created laws. It's **illegal** to harm, feed, or touch dolphins in the wild. Many people are working to clean up the oceans too. This work will help the world's dolphins stay healthy.

Dolphin Food Chain

This **food chain** shows what eats dolphins. It also shows what dolphins eat.

SHARKS

KILLER WHALES

DOLPHINS

FISH

SQUID

SEALS

communicate (kuh-MYU-nuh-kayt)—to share information, thought, or feeling with someone else

echolocation (eh-ko-lo-KAY-shun)—a process of bouncing sound waves off something to determine where it is

extinction (ek-STINK-shun)—a state where an animal or a plant has completely died out

food chain (FOOD CHAYN)—a series of plants and animals in which each uses the next in the series as a food source

illegal (il-LEE-guhl)—against the law

mammal (MAH-muhl)—a warm-blooded animal that feeds milk to its young

pod (POD)—a group of whales or dolphins

predator (PRED-uh-tuhr)—an animal that eats other animals

prey (PRAY)—an animal hunted or killed for food

rare (RAYR)—not often occurring or found

shallow (SHAH-low)—not deep

Books

Baines, Becky. *Dolphins.* Explore My World. Washington, D.C.: National Geographic Kids, 2016.

Loh-Hagan, Virginia. *Discover Bottlenose Dolphins.* Splash! Ann Arbor, MI: Cherry Lake Publishing, 2016.

Schuetz, Kari. *Bottlenose Dolphins.* Ocean Life Up Close. Minneapolis: Bellwether Media, 2017.

Websites

Common Bottlenose Dolphin
animals.nationalgeographic.com/animals/mammals/bottlenose-dolphin/

Dolphin Facts for Kids
www.dolphins.org/kids_dolphin_facts

Whale and Dolphin Videos and Sound
www.wdcs.org/wdcskids/en/videos_sound.php